LOVE, WHAT ELSE?

Thank you so much!

Melissa Proude

xx

LOVE, WHAT ELSE?

Poetry Collection

MELISSA PROULX

Contents

Intro

There are two things you must remember:

You're going to have a lot of loves in
your life & that's okay.

You don't have to say a lot,
to say a lot.

My First Love

I give you my heart
& you give me regret.

You couldn't even kiss me
goodbye.
As if you knew the reality
the whole time.

I was willing to fight for you
& you were not.

As my heart breaks
& shatters in a million pieces.
I hope others can appreciate this.
Appreciate my art.
Appreciate my words.
Appreciate my pain.

A person who is "in love"
with someone would
never abandon said person.

It's crazy how someone can do **one**
"bad" thing but a million "good" things
& still be punished for that **one**
"bad" thing.

Maybe it wasn't meant to be
But in that moment
I truly believe it was

I wish I could relive one memory with you
It's painful to think I might never find anyone
Quite like you

It's not because **you** were perfect.
It's because you were perfect for **me.**
We were perfect **together.**

It was a moment gone too fast,
A feeling...
I sometimes wonder if I will ever
experience it again

Smiles twenty-four seven,
That's how life was with you
That's how I wish my life was right now
Smiles twenty-four seven with you

You gave me **hope**
You made me believe in love
The love we so often see in fairy tales
You gave me **that**

If I'm not allowed to love you,
I will take all the love I have for you,
& love me more than I could ever imagine
I **will** love me more

Why?
Why must we be our best selves
To the ones who don't deserve it.

I guess my heart needs healing
I guess, time will heal it
because that's what they say right?
Time heals everything -
So, how much longer for my heart?

That is what I feared the whole time.
I feared **myself**

Healing takes time.
It's a beautiful thing.
It's beautiful in ways I cannot explain
It's a rebirth,
Like a butterfly or a lotus.

If you are doing nothing
but waiting for **time** to heal you,
You are only delaying the process.

I remember holding your hand
while crossing the street
Cold, but **happy.**
& in that very moment
I knew you were the one -
But it pains me now,
That moment was so beautiful...
I struggle with feeling either immense love
Or
Immense pain every time I think about it.

I was almost loved,
by the wrong person.

For awhile now,
I've been reaching & grasping
For love from others.
But when I didn't receive that love,
I threw myself into a downward spiral.
Into madness

You are worthy of all things beautiful
of all life has to offer
You are worthy of love.

Love with you was easy.
But somehow, there were so many things
that made it hard.
So I asked myself, is it really worth it?

I hope there are days
Where you feel like nothing can stop you.
The way you feel
When you're a child.
I hope throughout your life you feel that
Over & over again.
I truly believe you deserve this.

It was nice,
while it lasted.
You my dear,
You gave me hope.
You gave me just a taste
of what could be mine.
The only problem,
Is that it wasn't with you.

I see you in other people

Your face haunts me.
Today,
I saw you & felt nothing.
Now,
I give you peace as we both move on.
It's so beautiful to be freed from your pain.

What you need my dear,
is more love.
Surprisingly, you could have benefited
that from me.

& if I never see you again,
So what?

Sometimes I fee like I don't want
To let all of your memories go.
But this is a chance to create new memories.
With better people.
With better friends.
With better lovers.

What are you now?
Just a distant memory.
Someone I never think about,
Except only in what if's?

I don't understand you.
I know it's not my responsibility to understand you.
To understand your life & your family
I just wish you never let me be a part of it.
That unknowing,
That pain,
Is something I could have lived without.

Although I had suffered painful experiences
before you,
Yours was the most painful.

My Fake Love

It's impossible for one
not to be beautiful,
When one is smiling.

A tragedy
or
a blessing?
Only you have the power to decide.

The trees are blowing in the wind
& I feel uneasy.

It's not easy,
But I think that's the point.

I don't need your love,
But I will take it if you offer.

Just know,
Anything you want to accomplish in life,
you can by yourself.
You don't need anyone who doesn't need you

With you,
I feel imprisoned, in a cage.
With you gone,
I feel free,
free to shine to be myself.
To attract everything that will bring me joy & sunshine.

I don't wish pain upon you...
That is not my doing,
but the doing of God,
for you have created this pain yourself.

I know that I am magic,
I am sunshine.
You telling me this does not make it true,
but me believing it does.

I have learnt a lot from you...
But what I learned the most is that,
I don't need you
& I'm actually better off without you.

Ask yourself
why you are in pain
& also ask yourself
if the actions you've taken
have created this pain.

Is the way I treat others
also the way I want to be treated?

If you knew what I've been through
You would know
That I am capable of anything.

You leaving is the best gift
anyone has ever given me.
& for this:
I thank you.

Feel
Feelings are meant to be felt
& than meant to be let go

The things you have done
are irreversible.
& I know you already know that.
Because you told me yourself.

Do not act surprised
when people use you,
the way you used me.

When people tell you who they are,
believe them the first time.

You know what is never wrong?
Your intuition.
If you feel anxious,
there's a reason.

Listen closely,
if someone hardly listens when you talk,
they don't care.

If you want something done
You must do it yourself.
You cannot count on others
to do it for you.

I gave you too much
& you didn't give me enough

Leave me in peace
Not in pieces

The way you left is a clear message
that you never cared

I don't love you,
not after this.

Thinking about you is like climbing in a black hole
Darkness
& I pray I can come out alive
Breathing

Your memories haunt me.
You took me
& shaped me
Into whatever shape you liked
& I let you.
Moldable

My heart aches,
Once it starts
It's like it won't stop.

I see you,
& you send me in a whirlwind of confusion.

Let me remind you that your life can change
in just a blink
of an eye.

What is your super power?
Mine is **love**
& I will continue to give it
No matter what.

If you've caused me pain.
Don't feel bad
(I already know you don't)
Thank you for helping me grow
Thank you for teaching me that I am
far more superior than you.
Harsh.
True.

My Real Love

My heart is mine
I want you to experience it
But again,
it's my heart.

The thing that is difficult,
Is that we don't know how much
the other person is giving.
So, how much do we give
& how much do we take?

I need to protect my heart.
It hasn't healed.
If I go through more chaos,
I'm not sure my heart
would be able to recover,
this time

My heart is not the same
as it used to be.
& I **hate** it.

My heart is sacred,
I let you in.
You hurt me anyway.

Inconsistency is probably
one of the biggest
turn offs...

Words are just words.
Your actions add **meaning** to them.

I'm lost.
Who can tell me when it's safe
to be open & vulnerable?
Who can tell me when I need to
put my guard up?

You said everything I needed to hear.
I give myself to you
& I am left with the worse possible outcome.

Vulnerability
I feel so strongly about it,
yet I am constantly
sharing & opening up to
the wrong people.

I let go
I open up
& I crash & burn
I crash & burn
again
&
again
&
again

One day, it'll happen for you & for me
One day,
Remember.
It'll happen.

Aching.
I feel constant **pain** in my heart.
I have, what feels like an endless
stream of tears pouring out of my eyes.
Permanent wet eyes.
The paper I am writing on -
Drenched.
The ink from my pen -
Smeared.
Unreadable

Maybe it was the moon.
She likes to keep us up sometimes.

I fall hard
& then I scale back.

I want to share moments with you.
But instead,
I am having moments & your body is just standing beside
me.
Basically, what I'm saying is,
If you weren't there.
It wouldn't feel any different.

You're not a romantic.
You're a realist.

Life is about playing,
it's about having fun.
Especially this.
Especially love.

I'm torn.
"Just focus on you"
When the sun is out,
the birds are singing & the traffic is heavy;
the world is mine.
But what happens when the sun sets
& I'm left with myself & the moon.
It's you I think about.
How you're everything I don't want.
Not because I don't want you,
but because I want you & I can't have you.
Because you don't want me like I want you.
& that hurts.

I know there is someone
who is going to love all the "extra"
that I am & that I give.

It's mind blowing to me
that I am right beside you
& your hands aren't all over me.

I crave touch,
physical touch.
& you're telling me you'd
live on this earth alone?

I just want someone
who makes me laugh.
Who loves me gently.
Who whispers sweet things in my ear
when we are lying in bed on a cool & quiet
Sunday morning.

It shouldn't be this hard.
It should be easy.
Love should be easy.

No, it's not enough.
Carry me to the moon
& make love to me like I am
the most precious thing you've ever laid eyes on.
You've ever held.
That.
That will be enough.

I thought I'd be more sad.
I thought I'd be more broken.
But I feel more whole than ever.

You're not lonely.
You are free.
Change what you feel.
It's the same, isn't it.
Being lonely, **is** being free.

I hope you break down your walls.
Loving you is still such a beautiful thing.

It's not that I don't care.
It's that I can't be with someone who doesn't make me feel
like
life is actually laugh
& earth is actually sky.

There is freedom
in letting go.

You know that feeling
When you open the door,
Step outside
& feel the cool breeze on your skin
& the warm sun on your face.
That's how you make me feel.

You make me feel like a child
Happy.
Free.
Without a care in the world.
Solely focused on the moment right now.
Giddy.
Careless.

I can't get you off my mind.
& I don't want to say
"I can't wait for all the beautiful memories we are going
to create"
All I can say is,
what a joy it is to be surrounded by you
& how you make my heart dance
whenever I'm around you
& whenever I think about you.

I thought I knew how I needed to be loved.
But you love me in ways I never thought possible.
You love me in ways I can't explain
& it's just the most
beautiful thing.

What a privilege it is to be held
so gently by you.

The way you make me feel,
can only be truly felt
by surrendering.

The most obviously clear realization
It's you & it will always be you.
Unconditional love my soul will have
for you

It's like whatever I thought
I wanted out of love,
happened without even having to think about it.
Easy, just like that
Effortless.
The best kind of loves are the simple ones.

Acknowledgements

To my number one supporter, my love, my real love Ross Wilson. Thank you for everything, your constant love, your endless support. I couldn't have done this without you. You are everything to me and I cannot thank you enough. To my family, thank you for your kind words of encouragement and always believing in me. To all my loving friends, thank you for always being there for me and hearing me, I appreciate you all. An extra special thanks to my friend Joëlle Dahan for reviewing my book. I am thankful for myself, for not giving up, for being courageous in sharing my true words and for facing my fears whenever they arise. I can do anything.

CPSIA information can be obtained
at www.ICGtesting.com
Printed in the USA
LVHW040504030323
740633LV00001B/30

9 781778 033711